STUDIES IN ENGLISH L

General Editor

David Daiches

Professor of English in the School of English
and American Studies, University of Sussex

Already published in the series:

DATE DUE FOR RETURN

**This book may be recalled
before the above date**

General Preface

The object of this series is to provide studies of individual novels, plays and groups of poems and essays which are known to be widely read by students. The emphasis is on clarification and evaluation; biographical and historical facts, while they may be discussed when they throw light on particular elements in a writer's work, are generally subordinated to critical discussion. What kind of work is this? What exactly goes on here? How good is this work, and why? These are the questions that each writer will try to answer.

It should be emphasized that these studies are written on the assumption that the reader has already read carefully the work discussed. The objective is not to enable students to deliver opinions about works they have not read, nor is it to provide ready-made ideas to be applied to works that have been read. In one sense all critical interpretation can be regarded as foisting opinions on readers, but to accept this is to deny the advantages of any sort of critical discussion directed at students or indeed at anybody else. The aim of these studies is to provide what Coleridge called in another context 'aids to reflection' about the works discussed. The interpretations are offered as suggestive rather than as definitive, in the hope of stimulating the reader into developing further his own insights. This is after all the function of all critical discourse among sensible people.

Because of the interest which this kind of study has aroused, it has been decided to extend it first from merely English literature to include also some selected works of American literature and now further to include selected works in English by Commonwealth writers. The criterion will remain that the book studied is important in itself and is widely read by students.

DAVID DAICHES

Contents

Acknowledgement

The author wishes to acknowledge the kind permission given by Patrick White and Eyre & Spottiswoode to quote from *Voss*.

Note: Page numbers in brackets refer to the Penguin edition of *Voss* (1970). Works cited in the text are given in full in the bibliography.

1. The Preparation for the Expedition

Voss, the fifth of Patrick White's novels, appeared in 1957. Of the previous four, two, *Happy Valley* (1939) and *The Living and the Dead* (1941), are journeyman's work, while *The Aunt's Story* (1948) and *Tree of Man* (1955) show increasing skill and a decidedly more individual stamp. *Voss*, however, has from the beginning an inescapable air of authority and the assurance of a writer who has arrived. It is the first of a line of novels including *Riders in the Chariot, The Solid Mandala, The Vivisector, The Eye of the Storm*, in which qualities of largeness, uninhibited confidence and creative energy are unusually present. *Voss* is an historical novel set in the 1840s which, because of the overwhelming force of the protagonist and the human cogency of the theme, has an intensely living presence. The germ of the idea was presented to White by contemporary accounts of Leichardt's expeditions across the Australian continent. It was conceived during the London blitz, was 'influenced by the arch-megalomaniac of the day' and developed during 'months spent traipsing backwards and forwards across the Egyptian and Syrenaican deserts' (*Australian Letters*). It was also an expression of White's panic at what he saw as the Australian—but not only the Australian—exaltation of the average.

> In all directions stretched the Great Australian Emptiness, in which the mind is the least of possessions, in which the rich man is the important man, in which the schoolmaster and the journalist rule what intellectual roost there is, in which beautiful youths and girls stare at life through blind blue eyes, in which human teeth fall like autumn leaves, the buttocks of cars grow hourly glassier, food means cake and steak, muscles prevail, and the march of material ugliness does not raise a quiver from the average nerve. (*Australian Letters*)

The organization of *Voss* is clear and natural: the preparation for the expedition, the expedition itself in 1845, and then the aftermath of the expedition, a second exploration to explain the disaster of the first. But this straightforward scheme sustains a narrative remarkable both for propulsion and subtlety. These subtleties I hope to comment on in the course of my discussion of the text, but here I will say a word about the former quality.

Pace and energy are characteristic of all White's achieved work, whether in the early phase in *The Aunt's Story* and *The Tree of Man*, in the middle in *Voss, Riders in the Chariot* and *The Solid Mandala*, or the later in *The Vivisector* and *The Eye of the Storm*. They are qualities connected with an endless burrowing inquisitiveness, an incessant interrogation of many forms of existence, human and non-human. We sense in his best work an uninhibited flow and ease—not facility—of conception. The intellectual buoyancy which comes from this is all the more remarkable since on its other side his writing is notable for the effort to make every shade of being, every twist of character, every natural shape, dense and palpable. Thus, the drive in White's fiction takes in thickness of texture and activity of thought, solid detail and cogent speculation. Moreover, White refuses to dissipate his creative energy by truckling to the reader; accommodation is not part of his habit. He indulges in very little small talk, of which, indeed, he appears to possess a slighter fund than any contemporary writer of comparable significance. He insists on treating the subject invariably at the level which appeals to him, namely at its most serious, though not necessarily, as we shall see, at its unfunniest.

In keeping with White's domination of his material is his peremptory way with language, which is both poetic and aggressive. By 'aggressive' I mean not just an habitual lack of tenderness towards the language, but his manner of seeming to struggle with it in a kind of ferocious wrestling as though he were seeking to trip and force it to his purposes. If I say also that his way with words is poetic, the reader may wonder how this is possible when he often appears to be writing against the natural grain of the language. By 'poetic' here, then, I want to indicate the freedom White gives himself in respect of many of the common formalities of English, his wrenching of the syntax and his pushing its movements to their natural limits, as well as the choking thickets of metaphors through which he leads his narrative. And of course, to be both poetic and aggressive in this sense is by no means so paradoxical a combination as it may sound. White's effects when they are successful can be original and illuminating. The poetry is the consequence of the aggression and the aggression meant to strike out poetry from the language.

Here then are the opening lines of the novel, set in the Australian 1840s, of which the material is exploration, of which the theme is human experience conceived of as a dangerous exploration, particularly that profoundest part of it, in which the will grapples with the world outside itself, and of which the technique is poetic and exploratory.

'There is a man here, miss, asking for your uncle,' said Rose.

And stood breathing.

'What man?' asked the young woman, who was engaged upon some embroidery of a difficult nature, at which she was now forced to look more closely, holding the little frame to the light. 'Or is it perhaps a gentleman?'

'I do not know,' said the servant. 'It is a kind of foreign man.'

Something had made this woman monotonous. Her big breasts moved dully as she spoke, or she would stand, and the weight of her silences impressed itself on strangers. If the more sensitive amongst those she served or addressed failed to look at Rose, it was because her manner seemed to accuse the conscience, or it could have been, more simply, that they were embarrassed by her harelip.

'A foreigner?' said her mistress, and her Sunday dress sighed. 'It can only be the German.'

It was now the young woman's duty to give some order. In the end she would perform that duty with authority and distinction, but she did always hesitate at first. She would seldom have come out of herself for choice, for she was happiest shut with her own thoughts, and such was the texture of her marble, few people ever guessed at these. (p. 7)

Even from this short passage we can catch the unmistakable tang of White's manner and idiom. There is a beginning without preliminaries, an intense seriousness of attitude, an effort to render the experience dramatically and poetically, a creative curiosity which plays both on the squat, monotonous Rose, a minor figure, and on the sensitive and solitary Laura, a major one. In addition, we see the dislocation of the syntax, the naturally figured narrative, the employment, though in a way appropriate to prose, of rhythms one would think of as at home in poetry. That lopsided 'And stood breathing' conveys the anxiety and the heaviness of Rose's personality, just as her engagement upon 'embroidery of a difficult nature' and 'the texture of her marble' communicate the coolness and the fineness of Laura's. Moreover, as in a moment of conception, the law and logic of the novel are established, its world set up, its principals summoned, its development projected. The presence of Voss himself is implied from the beginning and the particular mark of his personality, his strangeness, his difference, made evident at once. A man, a kind of foreign man, a foreigner, the German; these phrases insist on the alien and external in Voss and prepare one for a character who will above all things be outside and beyond the ordinary run of mankind.

From the start, in order to establish Voss's status as outsider, White uses his instinct for the niceties of Victorian social conduct—perhaps an inherited faculty, since he himself hails from this increasingly minor minority, the established Australian gentry. The squat maid gulps at the sight of Voss. He is to be received in a room where Laura has been plying a delicate needle in complicated embroidery, a room which is 'rich and relentless', and which 'certainly gave no quarter to strangers'. When Laura moves, 'her silk Sunday dress sighs', and she observes how Voss, a bit of a scarecrow, who moves woodenly at the hips and speaks with a reckless lather of words in a blundering German accent, has frayed the ends of his trousers by walking on them. When he is given a glass of wine, the exact quality of which has been defined to the maid before ('not the best port, but the second best') he slops a drop which Laura Trevelyan pointedly refuses to notice. And yet we realize at once that the squirming discomfort of the shabby stranger, 'with his noticeable cheek bones and over-large finger joints', has nothing to do with any feeling of social inferiority. His is the unease of disdain. His seediness clothes the arrogance of an unnatural confidence. In his youth in Germany it had been intended that he should become a great surgeon, until he was 'suddenly revolted by the palpitating bodies of men'. Now he is sufficient to himself. 'How much less destructive of the personality are thirst, fever, physical exhaustion, he thought, much less destructive than people.' Their approach he regards as a threat to the integrity of his self and that is reserved for a peculiar destiny. Voss feels the menace of others and their capacity to be destructive of his self because the self for him is identified with will. We see, then, that one of the constitutive themes of the novel, human life thought of as the exercise of pure will, begins to be evident from the start, just as another central theme, the relationship of Voss and Laura, is intimated in their first uncomfortable meeting.

The impulse which Laura has to play the social game with Voss in this first scene, a game roughly ignored by Voss, resides in the more superficial part of her nature.

'You must excuse my uncle,' Laura Trevelyan said. 'He is still at Church.'

Her full skirt was moving across the carpet, sounding with petticoats, and she gave her cool hand, which he had to take, but did so hotly, rather roughly.

'I will come later. In perhaps one hour,' said the thick voice of the thin man, who was distressed by the furniture.

'It will not be so long,' answered the young woman, 'and I know my aunt would expect me to make you comfortable during that short time.'

She was the expert mistress of trivialities. (p. 10)

But in fact the characteristic effect of Voss on Laura's relationships with him is to strip them of any filmy social gauze and to put them at once on the most intense and serious level. Laura, it is clear, is a girl of intelligence and sensibility, who at the time she meets Voss is tortured by the possibility of losing her religious faith and who has been undergoing that Victorian crisis of conscience we see so frequently in literature and in life. She lived, of course, in a remote colony with no intellectual kinship, and Voss affects her, in her nervously sceptical phase, like lightning or inspiration or poetry. Thus, when she was with him she deserted the rational plane she preferred and 'her thoughts became natural and passionate'. Just at the moment during their first meeting when Laura is beginning to feel the effect of Voss as oppressive and enclosing—up to now she had been contemptuous of men and her Aunt Emmy feared that she was cold—there is a crunching of stones and leather, the smell of hot horses and then 'the terrible distant voices of people who have not yet made their entrance.' (p. 15.) (This is a tiny example of White's typical colouring of an event with the character's own feelings. Laura, it is intimated, finds the arrival of the others a menace to her intimacy with Voss, strained as it is.) When the Bonners appear, two thirds of the *dramatis personae* have been assembled, some of the main themes hinted at, and the way prepared for the natural introduction of the final third of the cast, the members of the expedition, who now begin to appear by name in the conversation; with these the great organizing idea of the expedition itself begins to assume definition.

The Bonners, their context, their presence, their quality and manner, vividly demonstrate Patrick White's sensitive historical imagination.

Their Sydney in the first half of the nineteenth century is an English provincial city set down on the Pacific shore, a strange blend of barracks, cathedral, and public gardens with the mysterious Australian trees and shrubs, the scurfy paperbarks, waxy camellias and gums, and hot scents and attentive silences. The Bonners belong to the mercantile class. They are touchy about their solid reputation, deferential towards their few social superiors, conscious of their obligation to those below them. They see property and wealth almost in a biblical way as the dressing of worthiness. Their respect for money is strong but not vulgar. They live in stone houses, their rooms are furnished richly and darkly, their men are drowsy after Sunday beef, their wives ambitious and conventional.

> They went into a smaller room that was sometimes referred to as Mr Bonner's Study, and in which certainly there stood a desk, but bare, except of useless presents from his wife, and several pieces of engraved silver, arranged at equal distances on the rich, red, tooled leather. Gazetteers, almanacs, books of sermons and of etiquette, and a complete Shakespeare, smelling of damp, splashed the pleasing shadow with discreet colours. All was disposed for study in this room, except its owner, though he might consider the prospects of trade drowsily after Sunday's beef, or, if the rheumatics were troubling him, ruffle up the sheets of invoices or leaves of a ledger that Mr Palethorpe had brought out from town. The study had flowered with Mrs Bonner's ambition. Its immaculacy was a source of pride, but it did make some people afraid, and the merchant himself was more at ease in his hugger-mugger sanctum at the store. (p. 19)

The physical presence of the Bonners is evoked as firmly. They stand on the middle rungs of a corporeal ladder, at the top of which is the spiritually finer Laura Trevelyan and at the bottom, ugly and unloved, the elemental, animal-like Rose Portion. Laura lives in her mind and on her nerves, Rose is hardly more than sentient. The Bonners themselves are thick in substance and assurance. Mr Bonner is complacent and, although uneasy in the presence of the alien Voss, puffed with pleasure at his status as patron and pleasantly excited by the envy of others. Mrs Bonner is limited and innocently snobbish. The comfortable husband and his commonplace wife are accompanied by their creamy daughter Belle and her red-necked athletically public-school young officer. In these lines from chapter one White catches exactly the madeira-cake quality of this world and conveys with an exquisite skill the whiff of its manners and spirit. There is a poetic excitement in the way he orders the names of different cloths to inform us of the tone of the Bonner world and its reverence for degree.

> Wealthy by colonial standards, the merchant had made money in a solid business, out of Irish linens and Swiss muslins, damask, and huckaback, and flannel, green baize, and India twills. The best-quality gold leaf was used to celebrate the name of EDMUND BONNER—ENGLISH DRAPER, and ladies driving down George Street, the wives of officers and graziers, in barouche and brougham, would bow to that respectable man. Why, on several occasions, he had even been consulted in confidence, he told, by Lady G—, who was so kind as to accept a tablecloth and several pair of linen sheets. (pp. 19–20)

In spite of the basic simplicity of the novel's design, the richly creative imagination of the author elaborates from the beginning an intricate web of relationships. There are those between Voss and the Bonners, those between Voss and Laura, those between Laura and Rose, between the Bonners and Laura and Rose, between Sydney society and the expedition itself, and increasingly between Voss and the members of the expedition. But all are subordinate to, or expressions of, the fundamental nature of Voss and the fundamental theme of the novel. The impulse of Voss's actions, and the inaugurating concept of the novel, is not any general belief or idea but the pure shape of the will, a force which has no content but only direction. The compulsion which Voss feels to cross the continent comes from the desire to fulfil his own nature or, more correctly and more narrowly, from the force of his own will. The conquering of the desert may seem natural to others for reasons of economics or geography or knowledge, or it may seem simply appropriate as it does, for example, to Mr Bonner, supplied thereby with the pleasures of patronage. Voss is willing to make any outward accommodation to such ideas if it helps him in his primary purpose. For him the expedition is a personal wrestling with the continent, and the continent is the only opponent his pride acknowledges as worthy of his will. 'Deserts prefer to resist history and develop along their own lines.' They have an intrinsic hostility to submission and they are therefore the proper target of Voss's will.

'Yes,' answered Voss, without hesitation. 'I will cross the continent from one end to the other. I have every intention to know it with my heart. Why I am pursued by this necessity, it is no more possible for me to tell than it is for you, who have made my acquaintance only before yesterday.' *[sic]* (p. 33)

The second phase of the first part of the novel is devoted first, to recruiting the members of the expedition and second, to extending and refining Voss's relationship with Laura. ('Recruiting' is perhaps too strong a term since it suggests a greater activity on the part of Voss than in fact exists. He is active only in the sense of being a naturally powerful magnet to which the others are attracted.) By this time the expedition is beginning to exist in plan and personnel, and the Laura–Voss theme has been unambiguously announced. The double subject will be elaborated and orchestrated throughout the novel. The assembling of the members of the expedition shows both White's intimate sense of the period and his Dickensian gift for infusing the minor characters with life. A phrase, a comic aside, a sentence or two, a glimmering perception, will suddenly enliven and individualize someone lurking in the margins of the novel.

Immediately before the 'recruiting' section of the novel, Mr Bonner is failing to persuade Voss to stay to mid-day Sunday dinner, 'a plate of prime beef and pudding'. These lines, from a passage dealing with a pair of hangers-on, illustrate the casual creative touch and the precise feeling for the temper of the period.

And there were the Palethorpes, who had arrived since. Mr P., as Mrs Bonner would refer to him, was her husband's right hand, and indispensable as such, if also conveniently a Sunday joke. Mr P. was bald, with a moustache that somewhat resembled a pair of dead birds. And there was his wife—she had been a governess—a most discreet person, whether in her choice of shawls, or behaviour in the houses of the rich. The P.s were waiting there, self-effacing, yet both at home, superior in the long practice of discretion. (p. 24)

'A moustache that somewhat resembled a pair of dead birds' and 'superior in the long practice of discretion' are phrases that might have been thrown off by Dickens himself. The image invoked and the temperament implied certainly testify to that kind of creative insouciance, as do the brief and speaking pictures of Topp, the anxious music master, and Mrs

Thompson—'Christian though she was, or hoped'—the owner and the housekeeper of the house where Voss lodges. Topp 'was a small, white, worried man, with small, moist, white hands, shameful in that country of dry yellow callouses. All he made was music, for which he was continually apologizing, and hoping he might not be called upon to explain what useful purpose his passion served.' (p. 30.) And as for Mrs Thompson, a decent widow, without encumbrances, 'certainly there were sons, but distributed, and at a distance' although 'her employer suspected the old woman of being the original Thompson'.

It is in Mr Topp's house that Voss interviews—this word conveys the detached, searching and sometimes disdainful way he communicates with the candidates—three of the first group in his expeditionary retinue. He does this in the intervals while he is examining catalogues, checking on tackle for the journey, eating a nice sweetbread for his supper, writing letters, abstractedly listening to Topp's music. His attention to his companions is usually subordinate to some activity or some introspection of his own. He appears never to be totally engaged with any of them, unless it be with the fourth member, Palfreyman, with whom he appears to have a relationship which is more nearly one of equality. And yet even with Palfreyman he is abstracted. 'He made quick, sucking noises to give Palfreyman the impression he was listening.' Voss is passionately concerned with himself alone, with his own nature and the realization of his driving purpose. Harry Robarts, a soft, powerful boy, is simply 'an easy shadow to wear. His wide eyes reflected the primary thoughts. Voss could sit with him as he would with still water, allowing his own thoughts to widen on it.' Voss even invites Frank Le Mesurier, a 'dark, young, rather exquisite but insolent young fellow', to join him in his expedition into the interior, since he senses in this young man, wrestling with his own daemon, some surrogate of himself. As well as the innocent Harry, the dissolute and snobbish Le Mesurier, the one who always loves Voss and the other who sometimes hates him, there is also the drunken Turner, 'a long, thin individual, whose mind had gone sour'. A certain cunning in Turner challenges Voss. Among these three there are relationships of suspicion and hostility, but in these Voss is quite uninterested:

'I am not interested in personal disagreements,' he said; 'who is drunk, who is a madman, who is disloyal. These are, in any event, of minor consideration. What distresses me more is my own great folly in continuing, like a worm, Frank, butting my head at whatsoever darkness of earth, once I have conceived an idea. You, Turner, Frank, are part of this strange, seemingly inconceivable idea. It distresses me that I cannot lay it aside, with all its component and dependent difficulties. But I cannot.' (p. 44)

Voss is one for whom external realities, even those of personal relations, sink away. He lives in an absolute way, not simply the possessor of an idea but possessed by it and indistinguishable from it. Even the way Voss falls asleep is used by White to illustrate this fact of Voss's psychology:

Voss went into the back room took off his clothes quickly, and without thought, lay rather stiffly on the bed, as was his habit, and slept. He fell, straight, deeply into himself. It was not possible really, that anyone could damage the Idea, however much they scratched it. (p. 44)

Palfreyman, the last member of the quartet gathered in Sydney, is another character who is developed, in a small space, to an astonishing degree of fullness and conviction. He has been commissioned by an English peer, 'a petulant one left over from a previous reign', to make a collection of Australian fauna and flora. In his life he balances two contrary devotions, one to science, one to religion, and his trusting nature builds a bridge between them in the form of a cult of usefulness, 'so that the two banks of his life were reconciled, despite many an incongruous geographical feature, and it was seldom noticed that a strong current flowed between'. (p. 46.) Voss finds in him a strength he is as yet unable to undermine, a strength which comes from the wholeness and integrity of his double devotion. Few are capable of doing what Palfreyman does spontaneously—simply neglect what Voss is saying to him and, by implication, ignore Voss himself and his overpowering will. An insect, glittering with all the colours of decomposition, is enough to distract him from the leader. Voss, when he looks at Palfreyman, is reminded of the old pastor of the Moravian Mission who once said to him, and without any suggestion of criticism, '"Mr Voss, you have a contempt for God because he is not in your own image."'

Already, then, the initiating concept of the expedition has begun to inform and shape the material of the novel; already the huge dimensions of the monstrous Marlovian figure of Voss are beginning to be suggested, a figure for whom it is natural to grapple with deserts and despise the Almighty. I turn now to the other principal subject of the first part of the novel, the relationship of Voss and Laura. There are four separate occasions on which Voss and Laura meet: at the Bonners' house when Voss calls on Mr Bonner, at the picnic at Point Piper, again at the Bonners, and finally at the quayside as the expedition departs.

The first I have already alluded to at the start of this essay. It is an encounter which deeply affects Laura, though in a negative rather than a positive way. She is unsettled, her feelings are distorted, the routine of her life broken. She is aware of being in the presence of something extraordinary. But she is not drawn to Voss: at first she hardly likes him, and even finds some aspects of him repulsive. Voss, on the other hand, is scarcely affected by their first meeting. He has difficulty afterwards in remembering the name of this cold and elegant girl, although he recognizes her features when he sees her for a second time. The four meetings provide a very modest basis for the immensities White extracts from them. But so powerful and penetrating is the treatment of the material that we come, rapidly, to accept the relationship as natural and convincing.

The second meeting, which takes place at Point Piper, is marvellously realized. It conveys the agitation of the children and the excitement of the day, while the miraculous quality of new life, weather, and personality are each quickened by it.

> The gay day of wind and sharp sunlight had pierced the surface of her sombre green. It had begun to glow. She was for ever flickering, and escaping from a cage of black twigs, but unconscious of any transformation that might have taken place. This ignorance of her riches gave to her face a tenderness that it did not normally possess. Many tender waves did, besides, leap round the rocky promontory along which they were stumbling. There was now distinctly the sound of the sea. As they trod out from the trees and were blinded, Laura Trevelyan was smiling. (p. 59)

The gleaming quality of the day and the radical change in Laura are heightened by the thick unspiritual quality of the men:

> Some of the younger men, with leathery skins and isolated eyes, braced their calves, and shook hands most powerfully with the stranger. But

two elderly and more important gentlemen, who would be Mr Pringle
and the unexplained Mr Pitt, and whose stomachs were too heavy, and
whose joints less active, merely cleared their throats and shifted on
their rocks. (p. 60)

In the 'theatre of light and water' Voss still shows the 'funny appearance
of a foreigner'. With a tremor of fury he realizes that 'mediocre, animal
men never do guess at the power of rock or fire, until the last moment
before those elements reduce them to—nothing.' (p. 61.) He becomes
aware of Laura as an ally and her feelings for him deepen and intensify.

She was too hot, of course, in the thick dress that she had put on for a
colder day, with the result that all words became great round weights.
She did not raise her head for those the German spoke, but heard them
fall, and loved their shape. So far departed from that rational level to
which she had determined to adhere, her own thoughts were grown
obscure, even natural. She did not care. It was lovely. She would have
liked to sit upon a rock and listen to words, not of any man, but
detached, mysterious, poetic words that she alone would interpret
through some sense inherited from sleep. Herself disembodied. Air
joining air experiences a voluptuousness no less intense because
imperceptible. (pp. 62–3)

Voss sees that Laura is not only his friend and ally but the one person
present capable of grasping the splendour of, as well as the peculiar flaw
in, his undertaking, its inhuman grandeur and its human meanness. 'It
was so calm now that they had rounded a buttress of rock. The trees were
leaning out towards them with slender needles of dead green. Both the
man and the woman were lulled into living inwardly, without shame, or
need for protection. '"This expedition, Mr Voss," said Laura Trevelyan
suddenly, "this expedition of yours is pure will."' (p. 69.) She understands that hidden in this crow-like figure, rusty and crumpled as it
is, is something of heroic proportions, something that might be ludicrous
if it weren't for his pride. 'His eyes were glittering with it in the mineral
light of evening.'

At the third meeting, a party given by the Bonners in honour of the
expedition, another Laura appears, a girl with a new, smouldering
beauty and a new and eager awareness. The dinner is served by the maid
Rose Portion, recently discovered to be pregnant, and by an elderly man

who has been lent by Archdeacon Endicott living in the same road, and who is a Dickensian person of awful respectability in a kind of livery and cotton gloves, only once putting his cotton thumb in the soup. Laura is now fascinated by Voss, even by his method of using a knife and fork. An immediate and almost painful intimacy blooms between them. 'He kept looking at her on and off, while she bent her head and knew that some kind of revelation must eventually take place, terrible though the prospect was.' (p. 84.) They walked outside after dinner, and their talk at once becomes personal and discovering.

> 'You are so vast and ugly,' Laura Trevelyan was repeating the words; 'I can imagine some desert, with rocks, rocks of prejudice, and, yes, even hatred. You are so isolated. That is why you are fascinated by the prospect of desert places, in which you will find your own situation taken for granted, or more than that, exalted. You sometimes scatter kind words or bits of poetry to people, who soon realize the extent of their illusion. Everything is for yourself. Human emotions, when you have them, are quite flattering to you. If those emotions strike sparks from others, that also is flattering. But most flattering I think, when you experience it, is the hatred, or even the mere irritation of weaker characters.'
>
> 'Do you hate me, perhaps?' asked Voss, in darkness.
>
> 'I am fascinated by you,' laughed Laura Trevelyan, with such candour that her admission did not seem immodest. '*You* are *my* desert!' (pp. 87–8)

They physical contact of Laura and Voss is very limited and correct, an occasional brushing of arms, an accidental bumping, and at one time even a modest embrace. But Voss senses symptoms of an extreme agitation or exhilaration in Laura and even, he is surprised to note, in himself. It is during this episode that the first encroachment is made on the closed system of Voss's egotism. This is something he finds he wants consciously to resist, but he becomes aware of other and more profound forces operating upon both of them.

> In the passion of their relationship, she had encountered his wrist. She held his bones. All their gestures had ugliness, convulsiveness in common. They stood with their legs apart inside their innocent clothes, the better to grip the reeling earth. (p. 89)

This meeting leaves in Voss the beginnings of a new kind of consciousness which, while it does not impede or constrict the stubborn and overwhelming force of his desire to conquer the desert, sets in train the transforming process which will work on him during his passage through the desert of Australia and of himself.

So he spent what remained of the evening. He himself could not have told exactly of what he was thinking. He would have liked to give, what he was not sure, if he had been able, if he had not destroyed this himself with deliberate ruthlessness in the beginning. In its absence there remained, in the lit room, a shimmering of music, and of the immense distances towards which he already trudged. (p. 92)

One quality of White's writing which I have not so far mentioned threads its way through this episode, and indeed others in which there is a question of manners or social context—namely a dry, malicious wit. It makes a welcome and tonic contrast to the brooding intensities which are more familiar in White. There are many examples, but let me illustrate it from the present episode by giving White's account of Mrs Bonner's management of her guests at the party:

Mrs Bonner, however, was creating groups of statuary. This was her strength, to coax out of flesh the marble that is hidden in it. So her guests became transfixed upon the furniture. Then Mrs Bonner, having control, was almost happy. Only, thought and music eluded her. Now she was, in fact, standing in her own drawing-room with this suspicion on her face, of something that had strayed. If she could have put her finger on it, if she could have turned infinity to stone, then she would have sunk down in her favourite chair, with all disposed around her, and rested her feet upon a little beaded stool. (p. 84)

In the final meeting of Voss and Laura, which takes place in public at the quayside as the party is about to depart on the 'first and gentle lap of their immense journey', there are other examples of the caustic and the comic, particularly in the sharp comments on Mr Bonner and Colonel Featherstonhaugh and other illustrious members of the community attending the departure.

Important heads were bared, stiff necks were bent into attitudes that suggested humble attention. It was a brave sight, and suddenly also moving. For all those figures of cloth and linen, of worthy British flesh and blood, and the souls tied to them, temporarily, like tentative balloons, by the precious grace of life, might, of that sudden, have been cardboard or little wooden things, as their importance in the scene receded, and there predominated the great tongue of blue water, the brooding, indigenous trees, and sky clutching at all. (p. 113)

Voss does not find the relationships with these puffy figures or with Mr Bonner so much distasteful as unreal. What he does find real, even if he feels he cannot pursue it, is his relationship with Laura. He hardly speaks to her but 'for an instance their minds were again wrestling together'. At this point Voss dismisses her from his thoughts and turns in a ferocity of concentration to the business of departure and the reality of the expedition. For Laura, the experience, ugly, untidy and painful as it was, has been the most important in her life. She is clenched in an intensity of bewildered misery. She has already begun within her mind the relationship with Voss that he will come to accept only during the transforming experience of the journey.

Patrick White is a sumptuously prodigal artist, loving the pure creative play or flourish, on occasion gravely to the detriment of his design. Yet he can, as in *Voss*, show himself to be a good housekeeper, managing his economy prudently and effectively. By the end of this first movement of *Voss*, a considerable amount of the work of the novel has been completed and the rest set in train. The dowdy town and the easy country around it, against which the harshness of the desert will be measured, are clearly in the reader's mind; the decent average of the population against which the ferociously extreme nature of Voss can be tested has been established; the relationship of Voss and Laura has been initiated, a relationship which, since they never meet again, will be carried on in the imagination of each and opened up to the reader by their correspondence. Several members of the expedition have been sketched with just the right degree of definition to mark them off as separate persons and yet to keep them united in a single party. And all the preliminary work on the gigantic figure of Voss is carried firmly through.

2. The Expedition

This most dangerous journey begins in the mildest way, with an uneventful sea trip to Newcastle where the company is met by Mr Sanderson; he rides with them through pleasant, easy country to his property at Rhine Towers which, with its homestead by the willows, store by the elm, cottages for the hands and a church in process of being built, is a triumph of civilized collaboration. Mr Sanderson's effect on Voss is to bring out that touch of malignant perversity which is an essential part of his nature—his original sin, as it were. As he rides with Sanderson, a cultivated and spiritual man, devoted to his wife, books and responsibilities, Voss assumes a simplicity of mind and an innocence of demeanour in a sort of silent mockery of his host. If I say mockery I may be suggesting too firmly that it is deliberate. It appears rather to issue from some deep ungovernable source in Voss. All but Mr Sanderson are conscious in some way of Voss's borrowing of Mr Sanderson's character. If the Bonners represented the dull orthodoxy which Voss detests, Sanderson and his wife and household represent a kind of civility and gentleness which is almost as alien to the German. It is this attitude which causes him on impulse to refuse beds for his company on their arrival at the Sandersons' house. He imposes on himself and his men this mortification to punish them and himself and confirm his distance from the kind of civilization embodied in the Sandersons. It is only Mr Palfreyman's collapse in the saddle which resolves this impasse at the beginning of their stay. During the confusion Voss and Le Mesurier accept quarters in the house while—an authentic contemporary touch—Turner and Harry Robarts are led off to the back by the grooms.

Two new members of the expedition join, a handsome, rich young man called Ralph Angus and a thick-set individual named Judd, an emancipated convict. Judd is a man whom one feels to be naturally good, just as Sanderson seems to be one whose goodness has been slowly and painfully achieved. Of Judd, White writes: 'He was, in fact, a union of strength and delicacy, like some gnarled trees that have been tortured and twisted by time and weather into exaggerated shapes, but of which the leaves still quiver at each change, and constantly shed shy, subtle scents.' (p. 133.) Voss does not object to Judd as a convict, as the conventional Mr Angus does, but he suspects him as a man. Judd's sort of goodness, like Sanderson's, inflames the evil side of Voss's egotism. It makes him feel uneasy rather than superior, it encroaches upon his isolation, upon the spiritual *droit de seigneur* he feels is his by nature. The convict had been tempered in Hell and survived, and Voss feels this may give him a hateful equality with himself. During their stay at Rhine Towers some of the men are encouraged by Voss's assumed fatherliness—a part strange enough for him to fancy—into revealing personal secrets to Voss, who receives them because 'they were valuable and because it repelled him to share the sins of human vermin on their infected wall. Yet that same disgust drove him to invite further confidences.' (p. 141.) Those who, like Frank Le Mesurier, do not confide in him, he will seek other ways to conquer.

During this Rhine Towers phase of the novel, Patrick White allows himself a degree of explicitness about Voss's nature, although no more than is warranted given the considerable amount of construction already completed. Judd finds in Voss a natural darkness and mystery in a way which suggests that the reader is being invited to share this view. 'And Voss, it would appear, was in the nature of a second monolith, of more friable stone, of nervous splinters, and dark mineral deposits, the purposes of which were not easily assessed.' (p. 136) The Wordsworthian element in his nature hinted at here is corroborated at various points by the evidence of a deep empathy in Voss with the natural process and the natural scene. He is often aware of secret and profound rhythms sustaining and expressing themselves in local phenomena. He is also shown to have Nietzschean leanings, as R. F. Brissenden has pointed out (Brissenden, p. 32). 'It had become quite clear from the man's face that he accepted his own divinity. If it was less clear, he was equally convinced that all others must accept. After he had submitted himself to further trial, and, if necessary, immolation.' (p. 144.) But Voss is saved from an unreal abstraction and given a genuinely human form by several touches: first, of managerial cunning (he rides out to Judd's homestead in order to learn from his surroundings how to understand Judd, although 'to understand' in Voss's sense means grasping and possessing and subduing); secondly, of flagrant and frantic contrariety (he is an expert in perversity); and finally, of cruelty and vanity in the way he treats his companions. If he is in some sense a Christ-like figure, he is one stained with the grubbiest kind of backsliding humanity. He has also a capacity for tenderness, all but stifled under his Germanic ache for sublimity, his puritan pride and obsessive will. It is a capacity revived by his experience of the candour and goodness in the air at Rhine Towers, a house which is a testimony to human trust and hopefulness. The night before the expedition is to leave he walks down to the river and is drawn nostalgically towards 'that strength of innocence which normally he would have condemned as ignorance, or suspected as a cloak to cover guile'. (p. 152.) He remembers Laura playing some insignificant nocturne at the piano and he realizes that 'it was in the quality of her rather stubborn innocence that her greatest strength lay'. (p. 152.) When he has finished his reports that evening and his pompous letters to patrons, he takes up his pen again and writes with an extraordinary intensity and recklessness. The tenderness is strained in this letter through his essayist's style and the stiffness and clumsiness of his personality. He expresses his overmastering purpose: 'The gifts of destiny cannot be returned. That which I am intended to fulfil must be fulfilled.' (p. 153.) But he also joins to it now the desire that Laura join him in thought and will, and he tells her that he will write to Mr Bonner formally to ask for her hand. This is the beginning of, or this creates the possibility for, Voss's redemption. Only a sinful man can become the redeemed man, only simplicity and suffering can be the conditions for the remaking of man, but all depends on the possibility of breaking out of the carapace of self. In the third section of *Voss* White writes: 'It was his niece, Laura Trevelyan, who had caused Mr Bonner's world of substance to quake.' Laura causes not only the thickly material world of Mr Bonner to quake, but the immensely more resistant spiritual substance of Voss's world to tremble.

The company then moves north across New England, in good weather and through easy country, to Mr Boyle's property at Jildra, the last human outpost it will come to before venturing into the unknown interior. The place and the owner are in the most vivid contrast with the Sandersons and Rhine Towers. The Sandersons testify to human effort and grace; Boyle is an aristocrat gone savage, living in a house like a warped skeleton, where 'smooth Irish silver stood cheek by jowl with pocked iron'. Certainly the place is a good preparation for the leaner, harder times ahead. Moreover, it is as though Jildra and Boyle, the squalid and the brutal, the Sandersons and Rhine Towers, the good and the sane, and the Bonners and Sydney, the complacent and the mediocre, together make up that whole range of humanity which Voss dismisses or by which Voss is dismissed. He is given in this phase not so much a Nietzschean grandeur but assimilated to a form in nature and endowed with a mysterious Wordsworthian existence: 'blackened and yellowed by the sun, dried in the wind, he now resembled some root, of dark and esoteric purpose.' (p. 169.) His companions continue each to hold on to things outside the control of Voss's terrifying will, e.g. Frank Le Mesurier to his poetry, Palfreyman to his science, Judd to the gear of the party and to the axes and knives which he oils with tenderness and care.

It is during this time too that we first encounter the blacks who are to play so significant and terrible a part in the journey. Their strange existence is marvellously rendered. The old native Dugald 'could have been a thinking stick, on which the ash had cooled after purification by fire, so wooden was his old, scarified, cauterized body, with its cap of grey, brittle ash'. (p. 170.) The younger one, Jackie, has the delicacy of a girl, 'listening with his skin, and quivering his reactions'. And finally we are made aware, while Voss is still at Jildra, of Laura. Voss is soured by distaste for the men he is with, 'blank faces like so many paper kites themselves earth-bound'. He repudiates his kinship with them. He humiliates Judd and scorns Palfreyman. But then he receives a letter from Laura, written in a cool, balanced and rationally analytic tone which still conveys the strange intensity of her feeling for him. 'Arrogance is surely the quality that caused us to recognize each other. Nobody within memory, I have realized since, dared so much as to *disturb* my pride . . . we have reached a stage where I am called upon to consider my destroyer as my saviour!' (p. 185.) His dreams are disturbed by subterranean memories of Laura. He tells himself, or something tells him in his dream or illumination: 'All human obligations are painful, Mr Johann Ulrich, until they are learnt, variety by variety.' (p. 187.) When he wakes he remembers whole lines from Laura Trevelyan's letter. He is not a new man but the possibility of renewal has been planted in him.

Laura, who is to be the agent of Voss's renewal or, to use an idiom appropriate to the system of religious metaphor which seems pervasive in the novel, the means of grace for Voss, is kept before the reader's attention by an economy which uses Voss's memories, dreams, and letters, and which also brings the affairs of the Bonner household intermittently into view. This is a method which simultaneously sharpens our sense of the isolation, the remoteness and danger of the expedition, and enables the author to develop the quality of Laura's feeling for Voss. There is a naturalistic context for the relationship of Laura and Voss. But of course it is a relationship developed poetically. On the slight physical substratum of their few brief meetings and messages, the imagination of each, moved by a deep emotional hunger, constructs a pattern of feeling and great delicacy and conviction. The fact that the relationship evolves with an intense and reciprocal empathy causes the reader no incredulity or discomfort because he senses an essential propriety between the nature of the experience and its poetic treatment. Patrick White requires of the reader a considerable degree of freedom from the logic of a straightforward representational world. But he has on his part the creative strength and the tact and realization which justify his calling on the reader for this sort of attention.

In the Bonner household itself, Laura appears almost as a Voss, that is as an exceptional outsider capable of spiritual growth in a society devoted to commoner, thicker aspirations. The maid Rose has been discovered to be pregnant and Laura's relations with her, which before were close but embarrassed, assume a remarkable intensity. She insists that Rose is to be kept in the household and not despatched to some institution. She brings Rose down from the attic into the spare room, 'the best room' as Mrs Bonner hisses in horror. She waits on Rose, engages a midwife for her, and prepares for her labour to take place in the Bonner household itself. When she defends Rose her eyes glitter and her hand becomes 'an ivory fist'. In fact she shows a version of Voss's will. But there is more than this. One begins to realize that Rose is having the child which is in some way Laura's, that Rose's is the physical pregnancy corresponding to Laura's spiritual one. When the baby is born it is Laura as well as Rose who undergoes the agony, achieves the fulfilment, and, in the ensuing days, the exhausted content:

> It is moving, we are moving, we are saved, Laura Trevelyan would have cried, if all sound had not continued frozen inside her throat. The supreme agony of joy was twisted, twisting, twisting.
> Then the dawn was shrieking with jubilation. For it had begun to live. The cocks were shrilling. Doves began to soothe. Sleepers

wrapped their dreams closer about them, and participated in great events. The red light was flowing out along the veins of the morning.

Laura Trevelyan bit the inside of her cheek, as the child came away from her body.

'There,' said the midwife. 'Safe and sound.'

'A little girl,' she added with a yawn, as if the sex of the children she created was immaterial.

The actual mother fell back with little blubbering noises for her own poor flesh. She had just drunk the dregs of pain, and her mouth was still too full to answer the cries of her new-born child.

But Laura Trevelyan came forward, and took the red baby, and when she had immersed it in her waiting love, and cleaned it, and swaddled it in fresh flannel, the midwife had to laugh, and comment:

'Well, you are that drawn, dear, about the face, anyone would think it was you had just been delivered of the bonny thing.' (p. 230)

When Rose dies it is Laura who keeps the baby and brings it up as her own, as she explains in a letter to Voss: 'Together with yourself, she is my greatest joy. Can you understand, dear Ulrich? She is my consolation, my token of love.' (p. 239.) In the course of the letter, which, when she reads it, appals the genuinely Victorian Laura, with its 'childishness, prolixity, immodesty, blasphemy, and affections', after describing Rose's burial she says, 'Finally, I believe I have begun to understand this great country, which we have been presumptuous to call *ours*, and with which I shall be content to grow since the day we buried Rose.' These words point to another theme which works its way in the rich undergrowth of this novel. It is that of Australia itself, or more precisely its unique landscape. There is in White an almost Wordsworthian sense both of the physical quality of a landscape and its spiritual suggestiveness. It is one of the unifying elements in the novel. At first the country through which the expedition goes has been comforting and easy or exciting and exhilarating. At the Sandersons and Rhine Towers there was a river valley with brown fish snoozing upon the stones, to get to which they had made their way through 'a gentle, healing landscape'. Now at Jildra it is beautiful in a wilder way: 'the wind bent the grass into tawny waves, on the crests of which floated the last survivors of flowers, and shrivelled and were sucked under by the swell.' (p. 165.) When Voss and Boyle ride out from the slatternly settlement, they begin to appear as mythical figures in one of those austere, mysterious canvases of Nolan:

> The two men rode on, in hats and beards, which strangely enough had not been adopted as disguises. In that flat country of secret colours, their figures were small, even when viewed in the foreground. Their great horses had become as children's ponies. It was the light that prevailed, and distance, which, after all, was a massing of light, and the mobs of cockatoos, which exploded, and broke into flashes of clattering, shrieking, white and sulphur light. Trees, too, were but illusory substance, for they would quickly turn to shadow, which is another shape of the ever-protean light. (p. 172)

During their time here the thirst both of the men and the country begins to be adverted to, although the pastures are still cool and the sky 'peacock coloured'. On the morning they leave Jildra 'the day opened like a square-cut, blazing jewel on the expedition, holding it almost stationary in the prison of that blue brilliance'. (p. 188.) As the day grows, they see the river dry and greenish brown pot-holes, and the vastness of the dun country. Voss becomes aware of the infinite Australian distance and, in balance with it, of the immensity of his presumption, and also of that other distance, the one between 'aspiration and human nature'. The expedition advances into this new country, where exquisite black spiders cling to their hair and the air is beginning to smell of dust, and where most personal hopes and fears are reduced until they are of little accord, and the men look back in amazement at their actual lives, 'in which they had got drunk, lain with women under placid trees, thought to offer their souls to God, or driven the knife into His image, some other man.' (p. 194.)

Life becomes grimmer and more extreme. They have, indeed, as Laura pictured them in her letter, 'left behind the rich and hospitable country . . . for some heartless desert'. Misfortunes multiply. Voss is injured by a mule, Turner is taken ill, cattle are lost and stolen, eating means swallowing a few leathery strips of the leg of sheep. The ground contains hardly a suggestion of leaf or grass or dew. And each member of the party obeys the logic of his own nature and responds to the sufferings of the journey in his own way. As I suggested before, each one clings to something brought from outside the expedition, some standard or impulse of memory supplied from a different life. Frank Le Mesurier is supported by his poetry, Judd holds on to the common kindness of the family man, and exercises it in tenderness to the simple-minded Harry Robarts, Palfreyman turns to his science and religion and his memories of his crippled sister, Turner and Angus, divided by class, to a common protective selfishness. Each of his followers keeps in tenuous touch with something from the past, while Voss is grappling with the question: Can he open himself to a human love which will not limit his absolutist will? When he writes next to Laura he has resolved that question. Although he has found human compassion a violation of privacy and an invasion of his own nature, he addresses her now as 'my dearest wife'. He recognizes that he cannot quite kill off his old nature and that he is 'reserved for further struggles, to wrestle with rocks, to bleed if necessary, to ascend'. (p. 217.) But he now understands that his is a true marriage. 'We have wrestled with the gristle and the bones before daring to assume the flesh.' (p. 217.)

During this phase we become more and more aware of the presence of the aborigines. These are the one form of human life utterly beyond the control of the human will. The blacks appear and disappear like birds or beasts. Their existence is purely a passage from moment to moment, answering some profound instinct for survival, and hardly directed at all by the conscious will. They drift across the landscape like smoke and are as responsive to the play of the physical life about them. One of the two domesticated aborigines, the ageing Dugald, is given this last letter of Voss to Laura, when he falls sick and asks to be sent back to Jildra. The old man rides away, in a trance of contentment, searching for roots and breaking them open to suck out water. His horse dies and he falls in with a company of aboriginals. In a kind of dream he takes from the pocket of his tattered coat Voss's letter:

These papers contained the thoughts of which the whites wished to be rid, explained the traveller, by inspiration: the sad thoughts, the bad, the thoughts that were too heavy, or in any way hurtful. These came out through the white man's writing-stick, down upon paper, and were sent away. (p. 220)

The letter is torn into pieces and thrown to the wind; the old man goes on with the blacks, 'walking through the good grass, and the present absorbed them utterly'. (p. 220.) What White renders so accurately and profoundly in these passages about the blacks is the other-worldliness of their existence. They do, strictly, live in another world, one which is the negation of active will, a projection of the appalling land, turning this way and that by some inarticulate sympathy with it. They survive by becoming part of the earth.

Phase 2

By this point in the novel the reader has become deeply engaged in the experience of the expedition, in its brutality, complexities and crises. And so powerful is the art with which it is rendered, so totally convincing is the realization, that the expedition naturally becomes a model of general human experience. Patrick White uses the psychology of the explorer as a metaphor of man. The explorer lives at extremes; he is constantly pushing back the frontiers of suffering and suffering is the universal experience of extremity which unites all men. Voss is the purest example of the explorer's psychology, but he is saved from abstract super-humanity by a grubby stain of backsliding man. There is a touch of malignancy, of the cruelty of vanity, in the way he treats his companions. When Palfreyman, a man of delicate constitution, who forces himself to the most menial tasks, is treating Turner's boils, Voss comments, 'Mr Palfreyman, in his capacity as Jesus Christ, lances the boils.' (p. 242.)

This is a fact of Voss's psychology which makes his final illumination possible and, when it takes place, authentic. Sin, as we have seen, was necessary before atonement was conceivable. *Voss* embodies Patrick White's perception of the conditions under which the remaking of man is possible: essentially simplicity and suffering. The suffering is sustained and terrible; the simplicity only barely and painfully achieved at the point of dissolution. It is characteristic of White's sensibility that such perceptions should so naturally find expression in metaphor. His work abounds in initiating and creating metaphors just as his narrative is conducted through choking thickets of imagery. Life as an unexplored desert, living as the experience of extremes, suffering and simplicity as the preconditions of man's most spiritual experience—this is the metaphoric structure sustaining *Voss*. There are other metaphors of this kind in the other novels: the heavenly chariot which is the intuitive, immediate, poetic consciousness in *Riders in the Chariot*; the glass marble in which enigmatic lights mirror the cloudy depths of personality in *The Solid Mandala*; art as the knife and the artist as the tormented but disciplined surgeon in *The Vivisector*; creative tranquillity in the midst of turbulence in *The Eye of the Storm*. It is in this play of metaphorical life that one comes to see or to feel most tellingly the lesson of White's art—the lesson, or the wisdom, that is, in Henry James's sense, which 'deeply lurks in any vision prompted by life'.

A second and more specific metaphor of this creative kind appears at the point when the cavalcade comes upon an oasis of water, grass, and butterflies:

> There was the good scent of rich, recent, greenish dung. Over all this scene, which was more a shimmer than the architecture of landscape, palpitated extraordinary butterflies. Nothing had been seen yet to compare with their colours, opening and closing, opening and closing. Indeed, by the addition of this pair of hinges, the world of semblance communicated with the world of dream. (p. 259)

The key phrases here are 'the world of semblance' and 'the world of dream'. The world of actuality, the expedition itself and its monstrous conditions and appalling effects, is, we ironically realize, 'the world of semblance' whereas 'the world of dream', the world of love and the ideal, is the world of another and more potent reality. Voss is tethered in the world of semblance, and it is his connection with Laura in the world of dream which offers the possibility of escape. Not only in the architecture of landscape but also in the architecture of people, the two worlds of semblance and dream communicate, modify, and fructify each other.

The transformation of the world of semblance into the world of dream, a constitutive theme in several of White's most important novels, for instance, *Riders in the Chariot* and *The Solid Mandala*, is present in a multiple and complex way in *Voss*. The world of Sydney and the Bonners stands to the total expedition as semblance to dream; within the Bonner household Mr and Mrs Bonner stand to Laura and Rose in the same relationship; and within the expedition the other members of the expedition are related to Voss himself in the same way; Voss himself is related to Laura as an inhabitant of the world of semblance to one in the world of dream. When the expedition breaks into two parties, the one consists of the convict, Judd, who determines out of a love of ordinary reality to turn back from the expedition, and Angus and Turner who leave it for wholly self-centred motives; the other, of Voss with Harry Robarts and Le Mesurier, all bound by Voss's will not to deviate in any way from his intention to cross the country. The first party is related to the second as the world of semblance is to the world of dream.

There is a strongly biblical and religious tone to the idiom and imagery in which the stumbling advance of the cavalcade is reported. The quality of this tone is not specifically Christian. It is rather that of an intensely religious spirit using Christian symbols because they happen to be peculiarly transparent to its meaning and because, in addition, they are most appropriate to the character of those early explorers upon whom Voss is based, as they are indeed to the German upbringing of Voss himself. After a night huddling in the shelter of the desert caves, morning dawns as a kind of Creation:

> The creator sighed, and there arose a contented little breeze, even from the mouth of the cave. Now, liquid light was allowed to pour from great receptacles. The infinitely pure, white light might have remained the masterpiece of creation, if fire had not suddenly broken out. For the sun was rising, in spite of immersion. It was challenging water, and the light of dawn, which is water of another kind. (p. 282)

The created earth becomes, as the expedition advances, 'the approaches to hell', 'devilish country', 'chaos', and is reported by Judd as he decides to leave the group, as 'Hell before and Hell behind, and nothing to choose between them'. When Palfreyman is instructed by Voss to go among a group of blacks to investigate the matter of their stolen axe, bridle, and surviving compass, he walks over the dry earth with 'springy, exaggerated strides, and in this strange progress was at peace and in love with his fellows'. (p. 342.)

> The aboriginals could have been trees, but the members of the expedition were so contorted by apprehension, longing, love or disgust, they had become human again. All remembered the face of Christ that they had seen at some point in their lives, either in churches or visions, before retreating from what they had not understood, the paradox of man in Christ, and Christ in man. All were obsessed by what could be the last scene for some of them. They could not advance farther. (p. 342)

The ghastly final scenes—the suicide of the poet Le Mesurier, the murder of the boy Harry, the beheading of Voss himself—are rehearsed with an increasingly religious language and reference, and the acts of destruction themselves are given a ritualistic function, something which, while it does not mitigate the horror, preserves it from being pointless and haphazard. The blacks are not simply murderers but priests of some other and incomprehensible god. The monstrous conclusion of the expedition follows naturally on the impulse which initiated it and the conditions in which it was realized. That pride should produce this result is perfectly in keeping with the fiction and theme. It is also the reflection of the ravaged harshness of Patrick White's reading of human reality. In other of his novels communities lust to persecute anyone or everything beyond the average, in the family the old persecute the young, the young savage the old, outside it men and women are locked together in malice. The whites despoil the blacks and the blacks destroy the whites. At the same time we are aware, in some novels more obliquely than in *Voss*, of the flow of love, of the possibility of illumination, of the conditions under which something rich and healing can be constructed. In *Voss* the relationship of Voss and Laura is the realized application of the double theme, and it is managed with the grace and conviction of a talent of a rare order.

That great and very different writer Henry James, writing of *The Tragic Muse*,[1] spoke of the presence in that novel of the *essence* and the *opposition*, and of the truth that their relationship would 'beget an infinity of situations'. The *essence* of *Voss* is the struggle of the will and reality, the effort of the will to impose government on both human and non-human reality, the two forms of existence which also constitute the *opposition*. That the human will cannot so manipulate reality is the truth irresistibly demonstrated by the experience of the novel. But reality, whether human or non-human, is not simply opposition; it also holds out to the will the possibility of redemption and life. This is not something which can be earned. It is not the wages of merit. Voss does not deserve Laura. She is a grace, a gift. Voss's moment of illumination and transfiguration in his death comes from his acceptance of this gift.

During Voss's agony, the Bonners and Sydney, 'an annexed and independent world', continue to offer to Laura a suburban version of his desert and a domestic *via dolorosa*. This is a point in the novel where freedom from realistically objective description which, as I said before, White's powers enable him to claim from the reader, is abundantly

[1] Henry James, *The Art of the Novel: Critical Prefaces*, ed. R. P. Blackmur (New York, 1934), p. 80.

justified. When a writer is thus gifted, he can, and the reader accepts that he can, permit himself a considerable degree of freedom from the logic of a straightforward representative method. The relationship of Voss and Laura has now progressed from its simple beginnings by means of a sympathetic parallelism into a 'fearful symmetry', a phrase I use to suggest that blend of life, terror and harmony which the relationship achieves in its final moments. Meanwhile, the Bonners in their kindly, innocent and philistine way are the uncomprehending observers of Laura's tragedy, and their external, half-oblivious relationship with her adds a degree of sharpness to her isolation and pain. This fact makes the Bonners more than simply engaging studies in complacent, decent dimness, and fits them to make a genuine contribution to the novel's substance and its technique. The use of the Bonner household for this purpose also allows White to employ his gift for satirical analysis, as for example in a devastating portrait of a smooth, fashionable physician.

Voss glides in and out of Laura's delirium just as she does through his. In fact, not only the borders between Voss and Laura, but those between different orders of existence are shown, under such intensities, to melt away. At the height of Laura's fever she feels herself struck in the face when Voss's horse throws up its head, and immediately after this while she is murmuring to Voss, White writes: 'So the party rode down the terrible basalt stairs of the Bonners' deserted house, and onward. Sometimes the horses' hooves would strike sparks from the outcrops of jagged rock.' (p. 358.)

3. The Aftermath

The final section of Voss, which begins at chapter fourteen, is a subtly ordered composition, in which the narrative lines cross and fold and straighten, in a design which is at once complicated and coherent. The tone and air are quieter, the manner more reminiscent, the pace slower. Three little girls are discovered chatting among themselves, and later with some adolescent girls, including Mercy Trevelyan, at a school at which, it appears, Laura Trevelyan is a mistress. There is the most natural and convincing nineteenth century sense about this passage, and one cannot praise too highly White's power of representation here—and indeed, throughout the novel—the conviction of his surfaces, textures and implied depths. The little girls and the older girls are precisely that, with characteristic attitudes and modes of expression. They are most vividly present. In fact, all the minor figures and the subordinate themes in this part of the novel, the mistresses and their snobberies, and those of the social context sustaining the school, are infused with the same springy vitality. They are both lively and enlivened by the author's creative curiosity.

One of the girls is invited to a party at which Colonel Hebden, a dry but impassioned Victorian explorer, will be present. The notion thus lodged will bring in Laura, the Bonner connections, and other ladies of Sydney society, as well as Laura's cousin Belle, whose own party at the end provides the occasion for the appearance of Judd, the one survivor of Voss's expedition. In fact, this last section is a muted repetition and reminiscence of the positive experiences generated in the substance of the novel. It includes an 'objective' description of the final hours of the aboriginal Jackie and an account of the disaster which overtook the three who deserted Voss, Judd, Angus and Turner; this follows not perhaps logically but certainly symmetrically on the conclusion of Colonel Hebden's second unsuccessful mission of investigation, and on Belle's splendid nineteenth century colonial party, where Miss Trevelyan, now the headmistress, reluctantly meets Judd.

When Laura, who is introduced with an exquisitely tactful

indirectness, does appear, we find her weathered by suffering, having achieved an equilibrium between anguish and lethargy. She has imposed on herself a 'rigorous exclusion of personal life, certainly of introspection'. In White's urbanely mocking account of the Misses Linsley's school, she is shown to be held in universal respect and, if considered too cold by some, others, particularly as White says, 'some blundering innocent', are constantly discovering her affection. When she is interrogated by Colonel Hebden about Voss, that remote but perceptive man observes beneath her detachment and reserve, 'a dry, burning misery', and when he meets her a second time at Belle's party, he brings Judd, the sole survivor of Voss's expedition, to talk to her:

> 'You know, Judd, Miss Trevelyan was a friend of Mr Voss.'
>
> 'Ah,' smiled the aged, gummy man. 'Voss.'
>
> He looked at the ground, but presently spoke again.
>
> 'Voss left his mark on the country,' he said.
>
> 'How?' asked Miss Trevelyan, cautiously.
>
> 'Well, the trees, of course. He was cutting his initials in the trees. He was a queer beggar, Voss. The blacks talk about him to this day. He is still there—that is the honest opinion of many of them—he is there in the country, and always will be.' . . .
>
> 'He was more than a man,' Judd continued, with the gratified air of one who had found that for which he had been looking. 'He was a Christian, such as I understand it.'
>
> Miss Trevelyan was holding a handkerchief to her lips, as though her life-blood might gush out.
>
> 'Not according to my interpretation of the word,' the Colonel interrupted, remorselessly, 'not by what I have heard.'
>
> 'Poor fellow,' sighed old Sanderson, again unhappy. 'He was somewhat twisted. But he is dead and gone.'
>
> Now that he was launched, Judd was determined to pursue his wavering way.
>
> 'He would wash the sores of the men. He would sit all night with them when they were sick, and clean up their filth with his own hands. I cried, I tell you, after he was dead. There was none of us could believe it when we saw the spear, hanging from his side, and shaking.' (pp. 443–4)

Despite the fact that this is the product of poor Judd's jumbled mind and clouded memory (which the reader is able to check against the documented deaths earlier in the novel), it still appears as a melodramatic analogy rather than a fantasy backed by some realized experience. The spear quivering in the side, Judd's vision of Voss's death and Palfreyman's, mars the crispness and effectiveness of this part of the novel and shows itself as a too obviously arranged and incorporated symbolism.

What is significant in this passage is the finding of both God and Man in Voss, an idea taken up by Laura herself. Voss carries the doubleness of human nature, which so fascinates White, to the point of genius. He is not simply good and bad, but God and Devil. This is one of the constitutive perceptions of Patrick White's work, the issue of the Manichean nature of his sensibility which throws everything into violent polarities: on one side the flow of love and grace, here exemplified in Laura and Palfreyman and in Voss's dissolution; on the other a stream of evil and loathing, expressed again in Voss's pride and abstract will, and in a lower way in Turner and Angus. It is not so much that White's sense of this truth about man's nature is original; it is rather that he feels it with such overwhelming power. His treatment of it, deriving from his vision of the violence of existence, of the intensity of being itself, has an astonishing energy of realization. White's reaction to life includes as well as this sense of its ferocious intensity a fierce disdain of the middling and commonplace, which, while arguing for a certain narrowness in the range of White's sympathy for human nature and experience, adds a personal engagement to his creation of Voss.

I began this study by pointing out that White's horror of the average was an immediate influence in the germination of *Voss*. The element of disdain in White's personality, which so exactly matches the pride in Voss's nature, makes the novel *Voss* in a peculiarly and intimate way Australian. In it White turns from the Australia of masses huddled in cities on the edge of the continent and devoted to the virtues of suburbia, to another Australia of infinite distances, paradisal light and unimaginable age, an impersonal and mineral Australia which is the apt nurse of heroic virtues. This Australia we experience through the eyes and the idiom of the stiff, displaced Voss. He is our telescope and our standard. In other novels White makes great play with the raw, philistine elements in Australian suburban life—he does this, in particular, in *Riders in the Chariot* and *The Solid Mandala*. They serve as a base line against which the reader can measure sanity, distinction and grace. In *Voss* a gentler, Victorian, middle-class and mercantile version of these suburban virtues is offered by the Bonners, and these compose a line against which we can establish the remote and desert-father-like heroism of Voss.

In this final part of the novel, Voss has graduated from the present into history, and that, it is clear, will in time assume the form of myth. Voss, and a central truth about, or experience of, Australia itself have become one. Australia is almost another character in the novel, certainly an impressive and influential force, the complex presence of which affects the organization and the feeling of the novel at many different points. Australia is the sole opponent worthy of Voss's will. The will to know Australia is the initiating impulse of the novel. It is Australia which appears in Laura's letters to Voss as the necessary and mysterious context and passion of Voss himself; and to know him requires her to experience the land. To experience here means not only, or not just, external or physical acquaintance. Rather, it is the mode of knowledge possessed by Jackie, the aboriginal who becomes a legend among the tribes:

> He became a legend amongst the tribes. Of the great country through which he travelled constantly, he was the shifting and troubled mind. His voice would issue out of his lungs, and wrestle with the rocks, until it was thrown back at him. He was always speaking with the souls of those who had died in the land, and was ready to translate their wishes into dialect. (p. 421)

Or as Laura says herself, at the end of a novel powerfully charged with the experience, the colour, and the significance of Australia itself:

> 'I am uncomfortably aware of the very little I have seen and experienced of things in general, and of our country in particular, . . . but the little I have seen is less, I like to feel, than what I know. Knowledge was never a matter of geography. Quite the reverse, it overflows all maps that exist. Perhaps true knowledge only comes of death by torture in the country of the mind.' (p. 446)

If the novel communicates the human significance of the Australian continent, if the expedition is an apt metaphor for the stresses of human life, if Voss himself becomes a lucent symbol of man and his struggle, this is because the country and the landscape are evoked with precision and solidity, and because Voss's complex, flawed and stricken humanity is rendered with marvellous actuality and fullness. He can be, in Henry James's phrase, in the preface to *What Maisie Knew*, 'the striking figured symbol' because he is 'the thoroughly pictured creature'. Eyre's *Journal* supplies White for *Voss*, as Shelvoake's *Voyages* supplied Coleridge for *The Ancient Mariner*, a work treating a similar theme with a period, a system of assumption, a protagonist, a drama and a context which powerfully attracted the author's profoundest feelings and unloosed that flow of unconscious forces of which Coleridge wrote in *On Poesy or Art*: 'In every work of art there is a reconcilement of the external and the internal, the conscious is so impressed on the unconscious as to appear in it. . . . He who combines the two is the man of genius; and for that reason he must partake of both. Hence there is in genius itself an unconscious activity: nay, that is the genius in the man of genius.' White in *Voss* displays the faculty Coleridge meant by genius here, and in addition he shows those gifts of management and discriminating skill which enable him to embody genius and make perception visible.

Sensitive as one may be to the imprudence of using the word 'genius' in relation to any contemporary writer, one still finds that the term offers itself quite naturally when the subject is a writer of the power and scope of Patrick White. Patrick White belongs to a line of novelists whose art embodies a concentrated and dazzling vision of man. Such writers are not manipulators of plot or cultivators of a sensibility or critics of manners or chroniclers of a period. Their art is initiated by their vision, and its form is determined more by a force from within than by any extrinsic scaffolding. It is somewhere between imaginative power and authenticity and crispness of detail that Patrick White's fails when it does fail, in the area where taste, calculation and the relation of means to ends are important. *Voss* answers such an account—impressive in the constructive idea, superb in its palpable concreteness, and on the rare occasion offering an imposed and gratuitous symbolism.

White's art at its most mature, and *Voss* is certainly one of the works that one would put in this category, is quickened and unified by the most powerful quarter of his sensibility, namely a concept of goodness which depends upon an unspoiled wholeness of the person. Such goodness, although it may be striven for, cannot be deserved. It is a stroke of providence or a form of genius, but in any case a gift, a grace, and one most likely to be found in the possession of those commonly regarded as blemished or eccentric or hateful, or like *Voss*, singular and extreme. In Patrick White's eyes the supreme gift of man, existing in a context of surliness, ugliness, and cruelty, is precisely the clarified consciousness that Voss attains only in the moment of dissolution.

4. Voss *and Others*

So far in this study I have concentrated on the text, its structure and significance, and paid scant attention to other critics. In this section I want briefly to present other views of *Voss*. This will have the double advantage of allowing the reader to decide among various and sometimes opposed reponses to the novel, and of bringing together material otherwise scattered, sometimes in inaccessible places.

Patrick White appears in 1961 in the bleached officialese of *A History of Australian Literature* as one of a number of rampantly unknown new writers. The historian acknowledges the presence in him of a considerable talent but finds him self-consciously sophisticated, affected, conscientiously unpleasant, and tiresomely reminiscent of Joyce. In sum, he is taken to be a considerable but spoilt talent. When *Voss* appeared in England in 1957 it was given an almost lyrical reception by the reviewers. The same was generally true of the Americans. Only the Australians themselves were dubious. Penelope Mortimer, as one can see from the back of the Pelican edition of *Voss*, was even moved in the *Sunday Times* to invoke the name of Tolstoy. While this erred on the side of hysteria, it was probably nearer the mark than the reaction of the Australian Ian Turner, who disliked the style in which *Voss* was written—'a parodist's pushover'—on the grounds that 'Australians are brought up to prefer the plain weaves of their own writers to the Gothic embroidery which is characteristic of *Voss*' (Turner, p. 74). The same writer sees *Voss* as a parable and Voss as an allegory for the historical Christ: 'Voss has his disciples, his persecutors and his betrayer; his agony and his reconciliation; his stigmata and his crucifixion. He is the divinity who humbles himself before the least of his servants. And he troubles the minds of men, and they record his legend' (Turner, p. 71). While Turner rejects the manner of *Voss* on account of its Gothic quality, he condemns the substance of *Voss* for its un-Australian note. The qualities which conquered the Australian continent, he explains, were human skill, hard grafting and a fair measure of luck. 'A rational realism is much more characteristic of our way of thinking than is the contemplation of infinite mysteries. For us, there is more tragedy—our sort of tragedy—in Rory O'Halloran, who lost his child in *Such is Life*, or in Tom Hopkins, who lost his youth in Lawsons's *Settling on the Land*, than there is in Johann Ulrich Voss, whose will was humbled in the Australian desert' (Turner, pp. 74–5). *Voss* must be rejected on this view because 'he is exploring, in an Australian environment, a mind, a way of thinking, that is foreign territory to most Australians' (Turner, p. 75).

Those who are not Australians, and no doubt some who are, will wonder what is the nature of this peculiarly Australian tragedy and regret that the mind manifested in Voss should appear to an Australian to be so uncompromisingly alien. White himself among his ambitions for this novel had placed precisely the opposite of what Ian Turner desired high on the list. 'Above all I was determined to prove that the Australian novel is not necessarily a dreary, dun-coloured offspring of journalistic realism. On the whole,' he said in 1958, 'the world has been convinced, only here, at the present moment, the dingoes are howling unmercifully . . .' (*Australian Letters*). It was in pursuit of this aim that White, who describes himself as something of a frustrated painter and a composer *manqué*, attempted to give to *Voss* 'the textures of music, the sensuousness of paint', and 'to convey through the theme and characters of *Voss* what Delacroix and Blake might have seen, what Mahler and Liszt might have heard.'

Robert Fry, another Australian critic, was offended not so much by the absence of the Australian spirit as by the presence of the Christian one. He finds the novel suffused by the more morbid aspects of Catholic mysticism, which project an unacceptably undignified conception of man. 'It conceives of man in isolation from man, selfishly working out his own salvation, giving nothing in human relationship except humility, and taking all in acts of penance' (Fry, p. 41). Remarks of this kind, and they are representative of certain Australian reactions, treat the novel in a savagely abstract way. Meanings torn out like this from the dense and figured body of the novel are so general, so detached, that they have little relationship to the concrete and realized work present before us.

On the other hand, it cannot be denied that White does fall into the error, intermittently, or perhaps only rarely, of pressing the symbolic sense too hard. An Australian critic, A. A. Phillips, calls this the algebraic use of symbolism, in which one has to state to oneself the equation $X = Y$, a process which disturbs the kind of response fiction demands. He finds this algebraic symbolism most apparent in *Voss*: 'Many readers—if those whom I have encountered are typical—seem to find some pedantic element in the book's structure softens the impact of the imaginative conception. In particular, that ghostly love-affair won't get off the page, won't acquire the flavour of an experience. . . . He here seems to be content if his reader intellectually receives the meaning he has set out to convey' (Phillips, p. 457).

As I have indicated in my own treatment, White's tendency towards algebraic symbolism is the consequence of a failure in creative and critical alertness and not an inevitable result of his method. Certainly his art, which is nearer the norm of the poetic than that of many contemporary novelists, is sometimes marred by this hankering after symbolic symmetry. But it is a fault of the moment rather than of the technique. Nor do I think A. A. Phillips at all right in arguing that White's characters have lost their freedom to grow since they are pushed and pummelled into predetermined positions. Voss himself is profoundly transformed in the course of the novel and so is Laura. And I cannot agree that White's method implies the existence of a long series of detailed correspondences between episodes in *Voss* and the life of Christ. The parallelism is subtler and less quantitative than this.

Symbols, myths and archetypal patterns are terms that appear frequently in the current critical account of White. No doubt this is in part the effect of the contemporary standing of this kind of critical habit, in part of White's gift, particularly evident in *Voss*, for dealing with profound and universal themes in an epic mode. Patricia Morley, trained in the school of Northrop Frye where criticism is primarily concerned with the system of ideas implicit in a work of art, and secondly with the images and archetypes which sustain it, finds that White's work relies not only on such writers as Dostoevsky and Tolstoy, Blake and Bunyan, but even more on the older traditions on which these artists drew, the Judeo-Christian-Classical heritage. 'Through the use of archetypes and images common to Western literature, White's novels obtain a richness of association, a cumulative power and an impersonal dignity' (Morley, preface, p. vii). She sees *Voss* as a modern version of the *Divina Commedia*: 'As in Dante's great epic, Voss's literal journey is both an allegory of the progress of the individual soul towards God, and a vision of the absolute towards which it strives' (Morley, p. 118). Patricia Morley's book, *The Mystery of Unity*, demonstrates clearly that if you begin with the idea that

Voss is a modern version of the *Divine Comedy*, you will undoubtedly be able to prove it. If in the course of your demonstration the body of the novel itself grows more and more invisible, so much the worse. Not that Patricia Morley's treatment is by any means the most extreme example of this method of approach. Her work exhibits a certain sense of proportion and some feeling for the texture of the novel. John and Rose Marie Beston have quite transformed the novel in their treatment into a contemporary *Imitation of Christ* or a doctrine of spiritual progression. They quote Laura's remark to Dr Kilwinning at the height of her sickness, 'How important it is to understand the three stages. Of God into man. Man. And man returning into God.' (p. 386.) This is important because, in the Bestons' view, Laura's statement about the three stages of man's spiritual progression, although they acknowledge it to be somewhat cryptic, enunciates the central theme of *Voss*. One can say of this, as one can say of Morley's view, that there is undoubtedly some notion of this sort implicit in *Voss*. But to abstract it in this abrupt and summary form distorts the shape and blurs the complex experience embodied in the novel.

A more modest version of the spiritual theme in *Voss* is given by G. A. Wilkes in his *Australian Literature: A Conspectus*: 'Voss leads an expedition across the Australian continent in order to mortify and exalt himself by suffering, as though in rivalry with Christ, to prove that man may become God . . . Voss seeks transcendence through a supreme egotism. What makes him so compelling a figure, however, is rather his vulnerability in this attempt. He must try to extinguish all human feeling in himself, not only by welcoming the privations of the journey, but also by repelling all emotions of fellowship—the suspicion that he may be thought to love his dog, Gyp, compels him to execute her forthwith' (Wilkes, p. 92). This plain statement has much to recommend it in its temperance and straightforwardness. It is developed in a more metaphysical way in an impressive essay by the distinguished Australian poet James McAuley in his essay 'The Gothic Splendours' (*Ten Essays on Patrick White* edited by G. A. Wilkes). He shows that *Voss* aims to produce effects more commonly found or attempted in poetry. He even suggests that *Voss* fulfils this aim with greater depth and more sustained intensity than most Australian poetry. McAuley sees *Voss* as a story organized around the contrast between the urban society of Sydney and the unexplored Bush: provincial gentility, commercialism, conventional piety, on the one side; on the other, the world of extremes in which concealment and compromises are torn away. Not that *Voss* relies on this too-simple contrast. The world of Sydney, for example, *is* the Bush, 'the country of the mind', for Laura. The Bush pictures an inner world that the urban man may enter also 'if he has the courage and metaphysical depth to explore his selfhood and his relation to God' (McAuley, p. 36). The conquest of a continent is the outward aspect of Voss's inward expedition. 'What Voss is dedicated to is the self-deification of man, to be achieved in his own person, through boundless will and pride and daring' (McAuley, p. 38). To be a self-subsistent, self-sufficient God requires one to abhor humility and to need no one. According to McAuley, White's novel is not simply the realization of a purely fantastic eccentric theme, the megalomania of an individual, but the use of this view to interpret imaginatively a tension within modern civilization. McAuley's reservation about *Voss* has to do with the 'wary evasiveness' with which this issue is finally handled. 'The Christian framework is assumed in the book for the purpose of stating the issues, and up to a point for resolving them. But in the last part the framework of interpretation seems itself to slip and become unclear' (McAuley, p. 45). McAuley's essay, which is one of the best accounts of the religious and metaphysical reading of *Voss*, finally blames Patrick White, it appears, for using the Christian framework instead of believing it. But this seems to me to misunderstand the nature of the artist's possibly unscrupulous use of whatever lies to hand in the way of means for helping him to realize his perception. I see nothing improper in White's use of the Christian myth. The only question is whether it is successful, whether his use of it is adequate for his artistic purpose.

It may well be that the reader will turn with some relief from these metaphysical readings of the novel, from literary criticism as philosophic tract or theological commentary, to something firmer and more specifiable. Systems of ideas and their accompanying sets of images and archetypes have a strongly volatilizing influence on any novel. Of course, ideas, philosophic and theological, do influence the form and tone of fiction but they are present in a more oblique and incidental way than the commentaries I have adduced would suggest. That the idea 'deeply lurks in any vision prompted by life' was the way Henry James thought of the existence of the idea in the novel. Let me therefore turn to a harder kind of notion about the novel advanced, for example, in a sensitive essay by the American critic George Core. He notes White's capacity to make the

far reaches of the Australian landscape come palpably to life. In his view
the country in *Voss* has a character as definite and individual as Hardy's
Wessex. 'The author not only incorporates the thickness of detail in
common life . . . but he can also render the feeling that the vast landscape
of Australia inevitably makes on the most casual observer. It is the same
dimension of vastness that one encounters in nineteenth-century Russian
and American fiction—in Tolstoy, Turgenev, Lermontov; in Cooper,
Melville, Norris. This sense of spaciousness and desolation is central to
Voss' (Core, pp. 3–4).

I should like at this point to refer the reader to some less enthusiastic
responses to White's work. Such a powerful and singular literary
personality is bound to intrude, sometimes harshly to intrude, into the
universe his fiction evokes. (We cannot make about White's work those
calm, formal distinctions which Eliot favoured between man and theme,
artist and suffering.) All of his novels, *Voss* no less than the others, bear
the indelible stamp of his personality, and comments made about other
novels may frequently be appropriate to *Voss*. George Steiner, for
examples, writes:

> The reciprocities of minute material detail and vast time sweeps, the
> thread of hysteria underneath the dreary crust, the play of European
> densities against the gross vacancy of the Australian setting, are the
> constant motifs of White's fiction. . . . (Steiner, p. 109)

He notes that in almost every one of White's novels and short stories there
is what he calls 'an eruption of savagery'. In *Voss* this eruption of savagery
is very much more restrained. If it exists at all it is in the deaths of Voss and
his party. But that is a development which issues coherently and naturally
from the situation. Other critics take the view that the domination of
White over his material becomes a form of cheating. Christopher Ricks
says of White:

> What was once the glory of the novel—its specificity, its
> knowledgeability, its being in possession of and putting you in
> possession of so much of the evidence (all of it?) on which you could
> judge for yourself—is at present the stunting impoverishment of the
> novel, since it is a permanent and well-nigh irresistible invitation to
> irresponsibility, to cheating, to the crucial immorality of the artist
> which Lawrence stigmatized as putting the thumb on the scale. (Ricks,
> pp. 19–20.)

While Ricks castigates the intrusion of White into his work as the putting of a thumb onto the scale, other critics react in a more favourable manner to that personality, particularly as it is shown in the prose, '[There] are few contemporary novelists' writes Peter Ackroyd, 'who have the fastidious eye and ear of Patrick White. His prose is instantly recognizable: it has a South American sonority and plumpness' (Ackroyd, p. 771). John Barnes, on the other hand, finds *Voss* one of the most dramatically effective of White's novels, but spoiled by mannerism, lushness and portentous mysticism (Barnes, p. 100). The dislocated syntax which many find intolerable in White, and which a famous Australian poet A. D. Hope once called 'pretentious and illiterate sludge', has by other critics been felt to be an individual and functional skill. Harry Heseltine in *Quadrant* (1963) maintains that from the time of his earliest work White has established a large fund of recurring interests which force their way into his prose as characters, situations and images, and that these are the spring of his style and the peculiar voice of his sensibility. People's hands, their skin, their breathing—the reader will remember Rose at the very beginning of *Voss*—are sensitive indicators of their natures. White refines, that is, from the grossness of a condition the subtlety of a mental state, a gift that has the fullest scope in *Voss*. White's presence in his novels and the language of their expression—the two topics which engage the interest of so many critics—are spoken of in a highly idiosyncratic but also enlightening way by the distinguished Australian writer Hal Porter. He speaks of the style as composed of 'razor-bright sentences, glassy clauses, vitreous jig-saw slices of paradox and poetry, the fastidious gluing on of sharp-edged fragments'. But beneath the glaze there are 'startling flashes, alert shadows, movement' (Porter, p. 1347). As to presence he says: 'Although perilously involved with his characters' wilful doings . . . he looms most, and mysteriously, on the outskirts of their curdled imaginations, a sky-line silhouette, blurred and ambiguous, yet immovably always there, creator and destroyer in one' (Porter, p. 1348).

Several critics have noticed White's stylistic adaptation to the matter in hand. For example, Barry Argyle, in an admirable critique of the novel, observes how White chooses two styles to convey the differences of intention and circumstances of the members of the expedition on the one hand and of Sydney society on the other. For those in the desert 'the language is filled with metaphor and the analysis metaphor presumes, to which is added some of the resources of the obsessed and humourless Voss's native German' (Argyle, p. 42). The language in which the Bonner group is described is much less poetic and self-revealing and more ironically dissecting. 'As they are without an ideal to which their lives can approximate, the author's commentary must provide one by which their limitations may at least be gauged and perhaps understood' (Argyle, p. 44). Laura, a member of the Sydney group, is with them but not of them. Her relationships, particularly those with Rose, are expressed in an idiom closer to that used for Voss and his company. The quality of the Voss dialect, spiritual and Teutonic simultaneously, is peculiarly German, as Barry Argyle comments. It is German in its mysticism, in its Nietzschean pretensions, and perhaps German too in a more repulsive, Hitlerian way. Barry Argyle's estimation of the novel is balanced and discriminating. On the whole he judges it to be a success. Another critic, Vincent Buckley, finds it ultimately a failure. He finds the concept magnificent but Voss himself grotesque: 'Voss's inner being is too nearly stifled by the weight of the analogies he is forced to carry' (Buckley, p. 422). Voss's spiritual state is brilliantly exhibited in the observed detail but White's persistent allegorizing finally dehumanizes him. The emptiness of the Bonner-Sydney connection serves to demonstrate the stature of Voss but in the end, in Buckley's view, 'it is the stature of a mission, a destiny, rather than of a man' (Buckley, p. 423). Buckley is profoundly impressed by White's capacity to bring such diverse kinds of human beings as Voss and Laura, and the lives they stand for, into a mutually enlivening relationship, but he is also convinced that 'there is something tainted about a creative habit which insists on an allegorical reading and then blurs the meaning it points to' (Buckley, p. 424). John B. Beston, in a decidedly more persuasive essay (Quadrant, 1972) than the other I have referred to (though not I think a wholly convincing one), analyses this essential Voss-Laura relationship in the novel. He finds it complex and confusing since in their meetings they show antagonism and rivalry but in their separation a mystical closeness. White, in order to show their isolation from the rest of mankind, glorifies their spiritual pretensions. They pass as mystics and fail as human beings.

One of those who finds the balance of allegory and actuality beautifully poised in Voss is R. F. Brissenden, whose brief note on Voss can be recommended on several counts. He stresses more than most the achievement of Voss as a historical novel when men 'particularly artists, intellectuals or explorers (and Voss is all three), seem, more often than not, to have seen their actions either in a religious light or in a light conditioned by the absence of religion' (Brissenden, p. 30). The imaginative truth with which Voss is realized as an explorer is matched with the skill in which the tone and manners of colonial society in nineteenth century Sydney are evoked. Nor does Brissenden accept, as so many critics do, that Voss is simply and brutally a 'Christ figure'. As Brissenden sees it, the Christian legend is an element, and a functional one, in the tale, and 'Voss always remains a novel, that is a convincing fictional representation of credible human beings, and . . . never hardens into the abstract over-simplifications of pure allegory' (Brissenden, p. 33).

Voss is also remarkable in showing much less grimly than White's later novels that sense of the nastiness of human life of which Patrick White seems to have more than his normal share, and which produces in a good deal of his work a flinching distaste towards the common and the raw in human life. John Barnes, in the essay already alluded to, makes this fact the principal ground on which he judges White. His impressive talent is thwarted, according to this critic, by a distaste for the subject matter of the novelist, namely human living. White's work reminds Barnes of Lawrence's complaint about Flaubert, that he stood away from life as from leprosy. Undoubtedly there are passages in White's later work which make it easy to see what Barnes means, and perhaps I may quote here what I wrote on this topic some years ago (A Manifold Voice, pp. 124–5):

We see in his work not only a positive but also a negative revelation. No matter how gifted a writer in Western society, even in so fresh and vital a form of it as the Australian, he cannot, it seems, help reproducing in his sensibility a certain failure of sureness or grasp in the contemporary experience of human nature. A neurotic twist or distortion, the reflection of a defect in our civilisation, forces itself into the work, even when, as with Patrick White, the writer is disposed by temperament and belief to a central and steadily traditional vision of man. . . . The statement of the artist can never be merely a comment; it is always in part the response of a participant. A sensibility so quick and inclusive as Patrick White's, however much it may be spiritually detached from the assumptions ruling contemporary society, is nevertheless bound, as it realises itself in art, to reflect not only the artist's individual vision but the radical disorder of the society it is turned upon.

In *Voss*, however, we are more conscious of the powerful treatment of the central theme, the human will and its transformation by grace, and other Whitean qualities. There is, for example, the unerring depiction of the quivering lesser characters. There is the sad, sour wit which brings decisively to heel colonial airs and graces. There is the strange empathic sense for physical objects and vegetable life. There is a gift for luminous generalization. And finally, one may note, White's predilection for the odd, the extreme, and the extraordinary—in this case for Voss and Laura—and his attribution to them, as a gift or grace, the possession of a special non-discursive mode of consciousness through which, in conditions of simplicity and suffering, the ultimate realities may be attained. And while one must not neglect to observe the features which mar *Voss*—the syntax bowled disconcertingly on the wrong foot, the passages which are too worked, too thick, too opaque—one cannot but feel, certainly I feel, that we are in the presence of a significant, peremptory talent. What makes Patrick White extraordinary is his power to discover and present Wordsworthian depths and distances. How reviving it is, at a time when the death of the novel as well as of literature itself is daily signalled, to find a major figure working with such confidence and power on a theme so large and so inclusive.

Select Bibliography

WHITE'S WORKS

Novels

Happy Valley (London, 1939).

The Living and the Dead (Toronto, London, New York, 1941; Penguin, 1968).

The Aunt's Story (Toronto, London, New York, 1948; Penguin, 1963).

The Tree of Man (New York, 1955; Penguin, 1961).

Voss (New York, London, 1957; Penguin, 1970).

Riders in the Chariot (London, Toronto, New York, 1961; Penguin, 1964).

The Solid Mandala (London, Toronto, 1966; Penguin, 1966).

The Vivisector (London, New York, 1970; Penguin, 1973).

The Eye of the Storm (London, 1973, New York, 1974).

A Fringe of Leaves (to be published London, 1976).

Short Stories

The Burnt Ones (London, Toronto, New York, 1964; Penguin, 1968).

The Cockatoos (New York, Toronto, 1975).

Plays

Four Plays (London, 1965).

Autobiographical Essay

'The Prodigal Son', *Australian Letters* vol. I, no. 3 (1958), pp. 37–40.

STUDIES AND CRITICISM

Peter Ackroyd, review of *The Cockatoos*, *Spectator* (22 June 1974), pp. 771–2.

Barry Argyle, *Patrick White* (Edinburgh, London, 1967).

John Barnes, 'A Note on Patrick White's Novels', *Literary Criterion* vol. VI, no. 3 (winter 1964), pp. 93–101.

John B. Beston, 'The Struggle for Dominance in *Voss*', *Quadrant* vol. XVI, no. 4 (July/Aug. 1972), pp. 24–30.

John and Rose Marie Beston, 'The Theme of Spiritual Progression in Voss', *Ariel* vol. IV, no. 3 (July 1974), pp. 99–114.

R. F. Brissenden, *Patrick White* (London, 1966).

Vincent Buckley, 'The Novels of Patrick White' in *The Literature of Australia* ed. Geoffrey Dutton (Penguin Books, Australia, 1964), pp. 413–26.

George Core, 'A Terrible Majesty: The Novels of Patrick White', *Hollins Critic* vol. XI, no. 1 (February 1974), pp. 1–16.

F. W. Dillistone, *Patrick White's 'Riders in the Chariot'* (New York, 1967).

Geoffrey Dutton, *Patrick White* (Melbourne, 1963).

Robert Fry, 'Voss', *Australian Letters* vol. 1, no. 3 (1958), pp. 40–41.

Harry Heseltine, 'Patrick White's Style', *Quadrant* vol. VII, no. 3 (1963), pp. 61–74.

James McAuley, 'The Gothic Splendours: Patrick White's *Voss*', in *Ten Essays on Patrick White* ed. G. A. Wilkes (Sydney, 1970), pp. 34–46.

R. L. McDougall, *Australia Felix: Joseph Furphy and Patrick White* (Canberra, 1966).

Patricia A. Morley, *The Mystery of Unity: Theme and Technique in the novels of Patrick White* (Montreal, London, 1972).

A. A. Phillips, 'Patrick White and the Algebraic Symbol', Meanjin no. 103 (vol. XXIV, no. 4) (1965), pp. 455–61.

Hal Porter, 'Patrick White' in *Contemporary Novelists* ed. James Vinson (London, 1972), pp. 1346–8.

Christopher Ricks, 'Gigantis', *New York Review of Books* (4 April 1974), pp. 19–20.

Carolyn Riley (ed.), *Contemporary Literary Criticism* vol. IV (Detroit, 1975).

George Steiner, 'Carnal Knowledge', *New Yorker* (4 March 1974), pp. 109–13.

Ian Turner, 'The Parable of Voss' in *An Overland Muster* ed. Stephen Murray-Smith (Brisbane, 1965), pp. 71–5.

William Walsh, 'Patrick White', in *A Manifold Voice* (London, 1970), pp. 86–125.

William Walsh, 'Patrick White's Vision of Human Incompleteness' in *Readings in Commonwealth Literature* (Oxford, 1973), pp. 420–26.

William Walsh, 'Fiction as Metaphor: The Novels of Patrick White', *Sewanee Review* vol. LXXXII, no. 2 (spring 1974), pp. 197–211.

G. A. Wilkes (ed.) *Ten Essays on Patrick White* (Sydney, 1970).

G. A. Wilkes, *Australian Literature: A Conspectus* (Sydney, 1969).

Index